The Bird You Barely See: A Quiet Philosophy for Living

By

Neil Holmes

Copyright © 2025 Neil Holmes

ISBN: 978-1-918038-72-9

All rights reserved, including the right to reproduce this book, or portions thereof in any form. No part of this text may be reproduced, transmitted, downloaded, decompiled, reverse engineered, or stored, in any form or introduced into any information storage and retrieval system, in any form or by any means, whether electronic or mechanical without the express written permission of the author.

I would like to thank Larissa for introducing me to bird watching and her immeasurable patience as I sit and write day after day. I would also like to show my appreciation to the two pigeons that regularly visit our balcony, which have entertained us immensely.

This book is dedicated to my mother, Vivien, and my sister, Jayne, without whom my life would not be what it is today.

Contents

The Sestina of the Bird You Barely See 6
Introduction 8
  The Bird You Barely See 8
Chapter 1 10
  The Art of Returning Home 10
    Home Beyond Maps 11
    The Wanderer's Circle 12
    The Pull of the Heart 13
    The World is Still Here 14
    Closing Reflection 15
Chapter 2 16
  The Patience of the Pavement 16
    The Art of Waiting 17
    Being Without Striving 18
    The Pavement as a Mirror 19
    Endurance Without Resistance 20
    The Gift of Presence 21
    Closing Reflection 23
Chapter 3 24
  Softness as Strength 24
    The Architecture of Softness 25
    Vulnerability as Power 26
    Endurance Hidden in Feather and Bone 27
    Adaptation Over Domination 28
    The Quiet Revolution of Gentleness 29
    Closing Reflection 30
Chapter 4 31
  The Grace of the Ordinary 31
    The Beauty We Overlook 31
    Living Without Applause 32
    The Sacredness of Small Things 33

    The Courage to Be Unremarkable 34
    Weaving into the Everyday World 35
    Closing Reflection: The Quiet Radiance of the Everyday . 36

Chapter 5 38
  The Gift of Wings 38
    The Lightness We Forget 38
    Flight as a Daily Ritual 39
    Freedom Without Abandonment 40
    The Courage to Leave and Return 41
    Wings as a Metaphor for Inner Life 42
    Closing Reflection: The Sky Within Us 43

Chapter 6 45
  The Fierce Love of Parents 45
    The Fragile Beginning 45
    Building a Nest in a Broken World 46
    Feeding from the Heart 48
    The Quiet Violence of Care 49
    Preparing to Let Go 51
    Closing Reflection: The Fierce Grace of Giving Life 52

Chapter 7 54
  The Language of Wings 54
    A Grammar Before Words 54
    The Choreography of the Collective 55
    Movement as Meaning 56
    The Skyborne Encounter 57
    An Invitation, Not a Command 58
    Closing Reflection: Not all communication is spoken. 59
    Not all connection is forged through words 59

Chapter 8 60
  Hunger and the Search for Enough 60
    The Oldest Language 60
    The Scavenger's Philosophy 61
    When Is Enough? 62
    The Appetites We Inherit 63

- The Beauty of the Small Meal 64
- Scarcity and Solidarity 65
- Hunger as Humility 66
- Closing Reflection 67

Chapter 9 68
Shelter, Nesting and the Search for Safety 68
- The Hidden Ledge 68
- Home for the Restless 69
- The Fragility of Safety 70
- Using What Is Available 71
- Between Exposure and Sanctuary 72
- The Gesture of a Nest 73
- Nesting in Chaos 74
- Closing Reflection 75

Chapter 10 76
The Fierce Love of Parents 76
- The Stillness That Warms 76
- Partnership as Protection 77
- Milk from the Throat 78
- Love Without Applause 79
- The Fear Beneath the Feathers 80
- The Silence of Continuity 81
- What We Learn from the Uncelebrated 82
- Closing Reflection 83

Chapter 11 84
Memory Written in Air 84
- Wings That Remember 84
- The Compass Within 85
- The Body Keeps the Way 86
- Remembering Without Story 87
- What We Forget and What Remains 88
- Carriers of Memory 89
- Memory as Belonging 90
- Closing Reflection 91

Chapter 12
Risk, Trust and the Leap 92
- The Moment Before Flight 92
- The Insecurity of Living 93
- The Necessity of Trust 94
- Risk as Aliveness 95
- The Flight That Finds Us 96
- Trusting Invisible Paths 97
- The Courage of the Small Leap 98
- Closing Reflection 99

Chapter 13 100
Fragile Bodies, Immortal Stories 100
- The Body That Endures 100
- The Bird in the Ruins 101
- The Memory in the Walls 102
- The Fragility We Flee 103
- Myths in Feathers 104
- The Story That Outlives the Body 105
- Closing Reflection 106

Chapter 14 107
The Wisdom of Non-Importance 107
- No one becomes a pigeon. 107
- The Ego That Doesn't Arrive 108
- Humility with Wings 109
- The Lightness of Letting Go 110
- The City's Companion 111
- Being Without Needing to Become 112
- Closing Reflection 113

Conclusion 114
- The Flight We Share 114

Introduction to the Companion Guide 116
- Søren Kierkegaard – The Art of Returning Home 117
- Marcus Aurelius – The Patience of the Pavement 118
- Lao Tzu – Softness as Strength 119

Brother Lawrence – The Grace of the Ordinary 120
Rainer Maria Rilke – The Gift of Wings................................120
Simone de Beauvoir – The Fierce Love of Parents 121
Martin Buber – The Language of Wings 122
Epicurus – Hunger and the Search for Enough..................123
Gaston Bachelard – Shelter, Nesting and the Search for Safety..123
Søren Kierkegaard – Risk, Trust and the Leap 124
Simone Weil – Memory Written in Air 125
Albert Camus – Fragile Bodies, Immortal Stories 126
Lao Tzu – The Wisdom of Non-Importance.......................126
The Flight We Share – A Concluding Reflection 127
References & Further Reading 129
   Primary Philosophical Works..129
   Secondary & Interpretive Texts.....................................130
   Additional Context & Inspiration...................................131
   A Final Word 131

The Sestina of the Bird You Barely See

The city never asked you for your wing,
nor offered you a perch but chipped-out stone.
And yet you stayed. And yet you made us see
the truth behind the silence of a name,
the cracks that thread beneath our bright-built world,
the dignity of dwelling half-alone.

No one applauds the creature born alone,
who learns to move with muscle, soot, and wing
across the scaffolded and bitter world—
who finds a heartbeat in the hollow stone,
who answers not to title, tribe, or name,
but listens to the gaps in what we see.

And what is flight, if not the will to see
a purpose in the pattern of alone?
You do not need the scaffold of a name
to lift your veined and iridescent wing
above the sprawl of ash and concrete stone,
above the billboards shouting out to the world.

You are not part of their ascending world—
you are the breath beneath it, they don't see,
the ghost that sleeps in vents and wakes the stone,
the minor god who lives and dies alone,
who answers sky with feather, thought with wing,
and shames those who stripped you of your name.

Yet even myths forget your shape, your name,
the ones who knew you guardians of the world.
We worship progress, not the pulse of wing—
we pave the past so fast, we cease to see

the hidden saints who shelter us alone,
who write their scripture in the cracks of stone.

I trace your path through city, flesh, and stone,
and every echo seems to speak your name:
not plague but prayer, not many but alone,
not pest but prophet of a fallen world.
The ones who own the skyline rarely see—
but you remain, and teach me how to wing.

Neil Holmes

Introduction

The Bird You Barely See

The pigeons live among us, and yet we rarely notice them.

They tread the cracked pavements of our cities, rise in sudden gusts of wings above our heads and nest in the forgotten ledges of the world. And then there are the pigeons found in the countryside. They rhythmically hum (or grunt) to the flap of their wings flying across open fields, and when they settle in an old village, they perch and coo on crumbling stone. They are everywhere, persistent and uninvited, existing quietly at the edges of our attention.

And perhaps that is why they are our perfect philosophers.

Living a life of being overlooked, belonging to no single place and yet being at home anywhere by adapting to a nomadic life without bitterness are impressive feats that many humans could never do. Perhaps they can achieve this through some form of wisdom, which we are forever seeking to discover within ourselves.

This is a book about pigeons, as it is also a book about patience, belonging, resilience, memory, trust, and freedom. It is about how an ordinary bird can carry an extraordinary meaning, if only we slow down enough to notice.

Pigeons have travelled alongside humanity for thousands of years. They have been messengers in times of war, used as symbols of peace and companions to emperors and commoners alike. Yet they ask nothing from us. We have given them no applause for all that they have done for us, and there is no monument to their loyalty. Yet, they are still here, thanks to their unique survival strategies that allow them to adapt and thrive in spaces we believe belong only to us.

Science has studied their remarkable instincts to navigate unseen paths, recognise human faces and return home across impossible distances. There is something beyond its biological nature: something poetic and philosophical can be glimpsed more clearly within its inner world than in instruments and graphs. This is a quiet invitation to remember what it means to live lightly in the world by trusting the invisible currents of life through endurance and with grace.

Throughout this book, we will explore the diverse landscapes of a pigeon's existence, from the bustling city streets to the high cliff ledges where their ancestors first took flight. Along the way, we will meet ideas from Stoicism, Taoism, Existentialism, and other philosophies that whisper in the same language pigeons seem to know by heart.

Maybe, thankfully, this isn't a book of strict lessons or heavy theories. It is more like a walk through a familiar town, seeing it perhaps for the first time through the eyes of a creature who has mastered the art of belonging by simply getting along with it, by enduring where others would falter.

Perhaps there is a lesson there for us, too.

I'm sure you have sat quietly in a square and watched this small, sturdy bird tip its head toward the light, and felt, however briefly, a sense of something beautiful and whole. Then, you have already heard the beginning of this philosophy.

This book is merely an invitation to listen a little closer.

Chapter 1

The Art of Returning Home

At first glance, a pigeon seems aimless.
It circles the sky in slow, widening arcs.
It tilts and twists against invisible currents, unsure of its destination.
But then, without warning, it sharpens, banks and disappears into the horizon with unwavering certainty.

It knows.
It always knew.

Scientists call it the *homing instinct*.
Through centuries of experiments, researchers have discovered that pigeons can find their way home from hundreds to thousands of miles away. Blindfolded, relocated and confused, yet still, they return. They navigate by a map we cannot see: a symphony of magnetic fields, scents on the wind, the angle of the sun and the memory of mountains and rivers glimpsed in flight.

And yet, no instrument built by human hands fully explains how it works.
The deeper the investigation, the more mysterious it becomes.

In the heart of a pigeon, something *knows the way home*.

Home Beyond Maps

What is *home* to a pigeon?
It is not a house with a number,
nor a deed with a name.
It is a place of belonging written into the body;
it is a loyalty without explanation.

Philosophy has long searched for this same invisible tether, where,

- Plato spoke of anamnesis: the idea that actual knowledge is not learned, but remembered, as if our souls once knew everything and are now simply finding their way back.
- Taoism teaches that the Way (the Tao) is not something outside us, but we must return through simplicity, patience and trust.
- Kierkegaard described the spiritual life as a journey inward, a *return to the self* that has always been hidden under layers of noise and fear.

The pigeon, without philosophy, enacts this perfectly.
It does not reason its way home. It does not need certainty, only trust in the pull it feels.

What if our lives are not about endlessly constructing ourselves with more achievements, more identity, and more validation, but about remembering who we were before we became lost in all the noise that surrounds us 24 hours a day?

What if the art of living is the art of returning?

The Wanderer's Circle

When a pigeon is released into unfamiliar skies, it does not rush.
It circles.

These wide loops have puzzled observers for centuries.
Some believed the pigeon was panicking and confused.
However, a closer study revealed something else:
the pigeon was interpreting *the world around it*.

- Sampling the magnetic fields.
- Smelling the wind.
- Observing the position of the sun.

In its circling, it is not lost; it is *orienting*.

Humans often misinterpret their moments of circling.
We call it hesitation.
We call it failure.
We call it weakness.

Perhaps, like the pigeon, our circling moments, pauses, uncertainties and wanderings are not failures. They are the necessary prelude to finding our proper direction.

Rainer Maria Rilke once wrote:
"I am circling around God, around the ancient tower, and I have been circling for thousands of years... and I still don't know: am I a falcon, a storm or a great song?"

To circle is not to be lost.
It is to listen.
To prepare for the moment when the way becomes clear, one would think that it is in the mind, but in the body.

The Pull of the Heart

In experiments, scientists have found that pigeons will endure storms, exhaustion and starvation to return home.
Even when relocated to new places, some pigeons, if released, will try to return to the first place they imprinted as home, sometimes travelling hundreds of kilometres longer than necessary.

There is something in their nature that is stronger than convenience.
And stronger than comfort.

It is the same pull that poets call longing, that mystics call yearning and that philosophers call the call of the authentic self.

In our own lives, we often silence this pull.
We prioritise the straight line, the efficient route and the measurable goal.
However, sometimes, there is a quieter map within us; one that does not follow logic, but love.

The pigeon reminds us:

- The heart knows the path that the mind cannot explain.
- Not every step must be rational.
- Sometimes, to return home is not a strategy. Instead, it is an act of trust.

The World is Still Here

There is a final lesson in the pigeon's flight:
no matter how far it travels, the world it returns to is never the same.

New buildings rise.
Winds shift.
Seasons turn.

And yet, it returns anyway by adapting, adjusting and weaving itself back into the living tapestry of the familiar and the new.

Home is not a fixed point on a map.
It is a relationship with oneself.
It is a movement of recognising who we are, forgiving what we are and renewing ourselves where we are.

The pigeon teaches us that returning is not regression.
It is not failure.
It is not weakness.

It is a conscious, embodied act of life.
It is the wisdom of knowing that leaving and returning are not opposites because they are the same rhythm of existence.

Closing Reflection

As we step into this journey together, among the pigeons and the cities and the fields, let us remember:

There is no shame in wandering.
There is no defeat in pausing.
There is no failure in longing for home.

Life itself is a kind of wide, slow circle.
And somewhere, beneath the noise and ambition, the path home is still written into our bones.

We have only to listen.
And like the pigeon, when the time comes,
spread our wings,
and return.

Chapter 2
The Patience of the Pavement

They gather where the world frays.

Along cracked sidewalks, under the shadow of rusted railings, on the edges of markets where crumbs fall and as the shoppers' chatter fades into the background, is where the pigeons wait.

They don't do this with the fierce alertness of predators.
They wait with the solemn patience, breathing the same air as we do, yet somehow apart from it.

Most passersby do not see them.
Or if they do, it is with the flicker of annoyance of another bird underfoot, interrupting the rush of human urgency.

We might notice something else if we pause, even for a moment.
A being that has surrendered the frenzy of striving, without surrendering the will to live.

A lesson, recorded quietly in feathers and dust, about the resilient dignity of waiting.

The Art of Waiting

Pigeons know how to wait.

They perch for hours over ledges, telephone wires and battered rooftops.
They stroll in small, slow steps across the pavement as they peck randomly at invisible things.
They huddle in groups under awnings when rain slicks the stones with their bodies tucked in and their eyes half-closed in trust.

To the impatient human eye, this may seem like laziness.
As if the pigeon has forgotten its purpose.
As if it has nothing better to do.

Yet perhaps pigeons have remembered something we have forgotten.

In a world that worships speed, ambition and instant gratification, pigeons offer a radical and silent protest:
The world will unfold in its own time.
Food will come.
Warmth will return.
The moment will shift.

There is no need to exhaust oneself fighting every second.

The pigeon teaches us that patience is not the same as passivity.
It is not resignation.
It is the disciplined art of *trusting time*.

Being Without Striving

Humans have been taught that existence must be justified.

That every breath must be accounted for and every moment bent toward a goal and a proof of worth.
Even leisure has become something to optimise and to achieve.

But pigeons are not caught in this trap.
They *exist*, quietly and unapologetically.

If an opportunity appears like a scattered crust of bread, an open window-sill or a patch of late sun, they take it.
If not, they do not manufacture urgency where none is needed.

This is not laziness.
It is the wisdom of Wu Wei, the Taoist principle of 'non-forcing.'
To act when the moment is ripe and to be still when it is not.

Lao Tzu writes:
"By doing nothing, everything is done."

Pigeons live this.
They move with the flow of the world, not against it.
They do not exhaust themselves chasing illusions.
They inhabit the rhythm of reality.

In a sense, they also embody the existentialists' dream of being without self-deception and inhabiting one's place in the world without masks or grand narratives.

Standing on the patient pavement, the pigeon teaches that being alive is enough.

The Pavement as a Mirror

The cracked pavement, the broken tiles and the stained concrete; none of it matters to the pigeon.

It is not the glamour of the place that gives it meaning.
It is the simple fact of *being there*, alive by breathing and perceiving what is around them.

The pigeon transforms even the ugliest patch of ground into a home, a field or a waiting place.

Perhaps we, too, demand too much from the world.
We tell ourselves we will be at peace when the scenery is perfect, the conditions are ideal, the noise ceases, and the cracks are filled.

But pigeons know better.
Meaning is not hidden in perfection.
It is hidden in the presence of being.

The pigeon standing on a forgotten slab of concrete with a patient blink at the world that reminds us:
Life is happening even here.
Even now.
Even on the broken stones.

There is no need to wait for a better stage before we begin to live.

Endurance Without Resistance

Pigeons endure what most creatures would flee.

The endless roar of traffic.
The indifference of millions of rushing feet.
The biting winters where the city becomes a steel trap of cold.

They do not resist these hardships with anger.
Nor do they romanticise them.
They continue.

Stoic by necessity, pigeons show us endurance is not about grim clenching of teeth.
It is the flexibility to adapt without losing one's inner softness.

Historical records indicate that pigeons have survived wars, famines and the collapse of cities.
Pigeons roosted in the ruins of bombed-out cities during World War II by finding warmth among shattered walls and nesting in the skeletons of what once were cathedrals and universities.

To endure, for a pigeon, is not to harden.
It is to bend and to adapt by finding the cracks where life can still grow.

We, too, often imagine that endurance must be grim and proud and that survival is a battle scar we must display.
But pigeons teach a quieter truth:
Survival is not about pride.
It is about gentleness within hardship.
It is about carrying one's small heart through the fire and finding space for trust.

The Gift of Presence

There is a certain grace in how pigeons inhabit their spaces.

They are not future-haunted.

They do not carry anxiety about tomorrow's storms or yesterday's scarcity.

They watch.
They breathe.
They respond.

Presence is their true strength.

To be present, truly present, is to surrender the illusion of control.

It is to give oneself entirely to the moment, whether that moment is radiant or grimy.

When a pigeon stands quietly on the pavement, it becomes a part of the living world.

It is not separate from everything and does not strive for a particular goal. It is woven into the soft fabric of existence.

And we, who pride ourselves on consciousness, intellect, and the endless refinement of thought, how often do we miss the simple miracle of standing still, yet awake in the world without needing to change it?

The pigeon invites us:

- To rest without guilt.
- To wait without fear.
- To breathe without rushing toward the next thing.

In every quiet moment of patience, we can return to ourselves, not as unfinished projects, but as beings already complete.

Closing Reflection

If you walk through a crowded square tomorrow, look down.
Not just at the grand façades, the flashing advertisements and the human parades.
Look for the small, patient grey figures with the pigeons standing quietly amid the hustle and bustle.

There, in the overlooked, is a different kind of power.
Not the loud force of ambition.
Not the brittle pride of conquest.
But the soft, fierce dignity of *being enough*, exactly where you are.

Sometimes, wisdom is not about soaring above the world; it's about being grounded in reality.
Wisdom is about standing quietly on the worn and cracked pavement while we continue to breathe, waiting and living as life demands.

That is precisely as the world is.
That is precisely as we are.

Chapter 3

Softness as Strength

In a world that worships hardness, of rigid bodies, hard minds and hard willpower, softness is easily mistaken for weakness.

From an early age, we are taught to toughen up and shield ourselves from adversity so that we can strike back before we are hit. We are told that survival belongs to the fittest.

Yet, pigeons, who are delicately boned and are vulnerable to the world's harshness, have survived longer than empires, longer than monuments, longer than most of the creatures who roared louder or stood taller.

Their secret is not hardness.
It is softness.
Adaptability.
Resilience is woven from gentleness and not brute force.

In the pigeon's soft body, we find a quiet philosophy: True strength is not the ability to resist the world but the ability to yield, move with it and remain unbroken.

The Architecture of Softness

The pigeon's body is a marvel of delicate engineering.

Its hollow bones, lightweight and airy, allow for effortless flight. Its feathers, fine and flexible, shield against wind, rain and sudden temperature changes.

Its muscles, though small, are tuned precisely for endurance, not for crushing or tearing.

There is nothing in the pigeon's design that speaks of brute dominance.
Instead, everything speaks of *adaptability*.

Where larger, heavier creatures perish when conditions shift, pigeons survive because they do not rigidly resist change.
They flow with it.

Their very softness allows them to endure storms, hunger, and the cold, which enables them to remain indifferent.

As the Tao Te Ching says:
"Nothing in the world is softer and weaker than water, yet nothing surpasses it in overcoming the hard and strong."

The pigeon is a living embodiment of this ancient truth:
Strength through suppleness.
Power through humility.
Victory through yielding.

Vulnerability as Power

We tend to fear vulnerability.

We shield our hearts and disguise our emotions with other behaviours because we fear that being soft invites defeat.
In a culture that prizes invulnerability, pigeons seem like poor contestants.

And yet, they persist.
In fact, they thrive.

Their 'vulnerability' is not a weakness; instead, it is a doorway to adaptability.
Because pigeons are not obsessed with invulnerability, they can move lightly through a constantly changing world.
They find new spaces when old ones close.
They discover new foods when old sources dry up.
They do not cling to one perfect plan; instead, they adjust, yield and adapt to life's demands.

To be vulnerable is to be open to change.
To be vulnerable is to be awake enough to notice the shifting currents and bend with them, not against them.

Human life, too, demands this kind of softness.
Hardness may protect us for a while, but in time, it cracks.
Softness endures.

Endurance Hidden in Feather and Bone

During wartime, pigeons were prized.

Their softness made them perfect messengers by being:

- Small enough to evade detection.
- Fast enough to outrun the dangers of the ground.
- Quiet enough to slip through the chaos.

Pigeons carried messages across bombed-out landscapes, through gunfire and gas, storms and hunger, all with the flap of a wing.

The irony is clear:
In an age of violence and machinery, the soft-bodied bird, the humble pigeon, succeeded where men and machines often failed.

Cher Ami, the famous World War I messenger pigeon, was shot, blinded and severely wounded, yet still delivered a message that saved hundreds of lives.
Through endurance rather than through ferocity.

Softness did not betray the pigeon.
Softness carried it, even through the fire.

There is a lesson here, whispered through history:
What looks fragile is often far stronger than it appears.

Adaptation Over Domination

Hardness seeks to dominate.
Softness seeks to adapt.

Domination demands that the world bend to one's will.
Adaptation finds a way to live within the world as it is.

Pigeons do not demand ideal conditions.
They do not need perfect forests or manicured gardens.
They thrive in what exists:

- On city squares full of footsteps and crumbs.
- Under bridges echoing with cars and trains.
- In forgotten attics and on crumbling balconies.

Their gift is not to remake the world, but to find life within it.

This adaptability is not a defeat.
It is a more resounding triumph, a victory of *coexistence* rather than conquest.

It is resilience without violence.

We, too, are often taught that victory comes from domination, from imposing ourselves on the world by forcing it to match our visions.

But the pigeon teaches a different way:
It teaches us to adapt is not to surrender.
It teaches us to survive with grace.

The Quiet Revolution of Gentleness

In an age of noise and violence, gentleness can feel almost revolutionary.

Walking and living gently allows us to approach the world with open hands rather than clenched fists; these are not small things.

They are radical acts of courage.

Pigeons, soft though they are, live this courage every day.

They raise their young in precarious places, on ledges with eaves exposed to wind and rain.
They forage without hoarding, taking only what they need.
They coexist with human indifference by never demanding admiration and never seeking to be more than they are.

There is a grace in this.
A small, persistent grace that says:
"I will be who I am. I will live where I can. I will survive, not by crushing others, but by weaving myself into the fabric of the world."

Ultimately, it may not be the hard or the loud who endure.
It may be the soft and adaptable who are more gentle-hearted who survive.

Closing Reflection

If you walk through the city tomorrow, take a moment to look around you. Look for the pigeon perched on a wire against the vast sky, balanced delicately against the wind.

Look for the small grey shapes moving between the pavement cracks. They live quietly and breathe patiently, being fully present in the moment.

Remember:
Strength is not always loud.
Survival is not always a battle cry.
Victory is not always a conquest.

Sometimes strength is a soft body riding fierce winds.
Sometimes survival is a beating heart hidden in a small, trembling chest.

Sometimes victory is the simple, stubborn act of being alive; still here, still breathing and still unfolding your wings into the changing light.

The pigeon is not mighty.
It is not proud.
It is not hard.

It is soft.
It is gentle.
It endures.

And maybe, just maybe, that is the greatest kind of strength we can aspire to.

Chapter 4

The Grace of the Ordinary

The Beauty We Overlook

They move through our cities like background music, unnoticed and uncelebrated, making them nearly invisible.
Pigeons drift across sunlit squares and cracked sidewalks, slipping between footsteps and the noise of the human world.

They do not dazzle with colours or shock with feats of grandeur.

They exist, weaving themselves into the texture of daily life as naturally as the rustle of leaves or the hum of distant traffic.

To most, they are an invisible mass of grey blurs in the corner of vision, often overlooked unless they beg or startle.

But to pause long enough to see them is to remember a quiet truth, honestly:
The world is alive with unnoticed grace.

It is not only the rare or the spectacular that deserves wonder. In it, there is beauty, quietness and constancy in the ordinary waiting patiently for our eyes to soften.

The pigeon reminds us:
Not all miracles come in thunder.
Some come on slow and steady wings.

Living Without Applause

The pigeon lives differently in a world that measures worth by applause, visibility and acclaim.

It does not ask to be admired.
It does not perform for approval.
It does not sculpt its existence around an audience.

It lives by breathing, walking, waiting and flying; to the pigeon, it is indifferent to whether anyone notices or cares.

This is not a defeat.
It is a deeper freedom.

To live without demanding recognition is to reclaim one's own life.

It is to belong to the Earth to breathe and to exist as itself, not to act to the shifting moods of others.

Pigeons are not lesser because they are overlooked.
They are not failures because they do not glitter.

Their dignity is intrinsic.
Their right to exist is unquestioned, even by themselves.

They are living reminders that the most actual worth is not assigned from outside.

It rises quietly from within, like the steady warmth of a small heart beating in the city's cold morning.

The Sacredness of Small Things

In ancient traditions of Zen, Taoism and early Christian mysticism, there is a thread of wisdom that runs quietly through the teachings:
The sacred is not only found in mountaintops or cathedrals.
It is hidden in small things.

Zen has a saying: *Before enlightenment, chop wood, carry water. After enlightenment, one should return to the mundane tasks of chopping wood and carrying water.*

Nothing outwardly changes.
The miracle is in the seeing.

The ordinary, fully entered, becomes luminous.

Pigeons live this truth without knowing it.

- To rise with the first light.
- To wait with patience for what the day will offer.
- To breathe the dusty air of alleys and squares.
- To fold one's wings beneath broken stones and wait for rain to pass.

These small acts are not glamorous.
They are sacred.
They are acts of life woven into the tapestry of the world.

The pigeon teaches not through brilliance, but through persistence:
every breath, step, and waiting hour carries its quiet holiness.

The Courage to Be Unremarkable

Modern culture urges us to be extraordinary.
To stand out, rise above, and distinguish ourselves endlessly from the fabric of ordinary life.

But pigeons offer a different kind of courage: the courage to be unremarkable.
The courage to live humbly and wholly without the need to impress or dominate.

To be small is not to be insignificant.
To be common is not to be forgettable.

There is an immense strength in choosing to live deeply within the everyday, rather than scrambling for a life that sparkles but leaves the soul hollow.

The pigeon, existing without grandeur, its stillness touches the wind.
Stillness feels the pulse of seasons turning.
Stillness tastes the rain, warms itself in patches of sunlight and teaches its young the delicate arts of flight and survival.

It belongs not to applause, but to the world itself.

And perhaps that is the greater belonging.

Weaving into the Everyday World

Pigeons do not stand apart from the world.
They weave themselves into it, moving lightly through the spaces humans leave behind.

A patch of sun on a cracked bench.
A dry ledge beneath a forgotten sign.
A market square that smells of bread and oranges that have spilt out onto the stones.

Pigeons do not demand that the world be perfect before they live within it.
They find the seams, the openings and the overlooked places where life can still breathe.

This, too, is a wisdom worth remembering.

We do not have to wait for ideal conditions to begin.
We do not have to wait for applause to belong.
We do not have to carve out a space to live meaningfully.

We can weave ourselves quietly into the fabric of ordinary life by sharing breath with the city, moving with the day, and finding sanctuaries in unexpected places.

Closing Reflection: The Quiet Radiance of the Everyday

Imagine standing in the soft light of a city square:

Children chase the grey shadows across the stones.
Vendors call out in bursts of laughter.
The scent of coffee drifts through the air, carried on the gentle breeze.

And there, on the edge of all the movement and noise, stands a pigeon.

Not grand.
Not triumphant.
Simply present.

It watches the world without judgment.
It breathes without hurry.
It lives without demanding notice.

Its small body holds the quiet radiance of everything the world forgets:
The dignity of survival.
The miracle of breath.
The sacredness of simply standing alive under the changing sky.

In its plain feathers, in its patient eyes, in its uncelebrated steps, the pigeon reminds us:

There is grace in the ordinary.
There is holiness in the overlooked.
There is wonder stitched into the very pavement beneath our feet.

To see it, we need not chase the extraordinary.
We need only to soften our gaze.
To slow our breath.
To let the world reveal its beauty in the smallest, humblest places.

The pigeon knows.
It always has.

Chapter 5

The Gift of Wings

The Lightness We Forget

There is a kind of lightness that we often overlook.

It rises quietly into the air, folding itself across rooftops and trembling along the vast corridors of morning. It lifts itself into the slow spirals of pigeons gathering over a square, rising unseen into the breath of the sky.

Pigeons, in their everyday rising, remind us that freedom is not always loud. It does not come only in bursts of courage or grand departures. Sometimes it flutters at the edge of things, in a small wingbeat, in a brief circling above crowded streets, in a silent letting go of weight.

In a world heavy with urgency and ambition, the pigeon's flight is a living thread of something lighter; a quiet inheritance we, too, once knew.
The ability to lift without forcing.
The ability to belong to the sky without abandoning the ground.

We do not always notice it. But every day, above the noise and rush, small wings rise, reminding us that lightness has never been as distant as we imagined.

Flight as a Daily Ritual

For pigeons, flight is not a spectacle.
It is not a ceremony reserved for rare occasions.

It is woven into the texture of living; a daily movement as natural as breathing.

They rise without fanfare, slip between buildings, and circle through the dusty light. They tilt their bodies into invisible currents, adjusting without drama by trusting the air to carry them.

Flight is not an escape.
It is not a rebellion against the earth.

It is a way of being fully in the world and free.

Pigeons remind us that freedom does not have to sever us from where we stand.
Freedom can be a rhythm, a lifting and returning, a circling and belonging, a dance between here and there.

There is grace in flight made ordinary.
Freedom is woven into the fabric of everyday life if we move with it.

Freedom Without Abandonment

Pigeons do not flee the world when they fly.

They do not abandon the earth.
They do not renounce the streets, stones or small spaces where they find shelter, food and companionship.

They fly, but they also return.

They rise into the open air, feel the pull of the wind, taste the wide spaces above, and then descend again, whether to the ledge, to the square or to the place where their lives are woven with the dust and breath of the human world.

Their freedom is not a separation.
It is a relationship.

The pigeon teaches us that true freedom is not running away. It is moving deeply within the life we are given, knowing we can lift and return, wander and belong, and leave and love again.

Freedom is not abandonment.
It is the full inhabiting of space with the courage to move widely and the tenderness to remain connected.

The Courage to Leave and Return

To fly at all is an act of trust.

It requires letting go of the solid ground.
It requires leaning into invisible forces by trusting currents that cannot be seen, only felt.

When pigeons rise from a square, there is a moment where the world falls away beneath them, where gravity loosens and the great uncertain air becomes home.

And yet they do not fear it.
They do not hesitate endlessly at the edge of movement.
They rise lightly, entirely and allow themselves to be carried.

And after the flight, they return.

To leave and return is one of the oldest rhythms of life.
It is the journey of rivers meeting oceans and circling back as rain.
It is the migration of birds, the shifting of seasons, the heartbeat of trust beating steadily against the unknown.

We, too, are called to move.
To step beyond what is certain.
Knowing we are not losing our home, we are expanding it into more expansive spaces.

The pigeon shows us:
Leaving is not betrayal.
Returning is not failure.
Movement is not disloyalty to the ground beneath us.
It is a form of love.

Wings as a Metaphor for Inner Life

The wings of a pigeon are not just physical.
They are metaphors for something every living being carries inside.

The capacity to allow ourselves to rise, not necessarily into the sky, but into moments of possibility, perspective, and hope.

We carry wings inside us, even if we forget them.
Wings that let us rise beyond despair, beyond stagnation and beyond the heavy certainties of fear.

To have wings is not to abandon the ordinary.
It is to be able to see from above, to glimpse new paths through the worn streets of our lives and to move freely within the familiar and the unknown.

It is to feel the wind in our spirit when the world seems thick with stone.

The pigeons remind us:
You can be small.
You can be humble.
You can live close to the earth and still carry the sky inside you.

Flight is not about glory.
It is about breathing wider.

Closing Reflection: The Sky Within Us

Imagine a morning in a city that is sleeping.

The rooftops are still cool from the night. The sun is a soft, uncertain light gathering at the edges of the sky. The world is slow, unhurried, and still half-dreaming.

A small flock of pigeons rise suddenly from a square, lifting into the new day.

No one applauds.
No one notices.
They spiral upward, not with fanfare, but with belonging.

They do not leave the world behind.
They move within it, brushing the early light and stitching the air into circles of trust.

And in that silent flight, a forgotten truth hums:

We were made for this, too.

We were made to live grounded and to rise.
To walk and to soar.
To move with the winds of change without losing the steady beat of belonging.

There is a sky within us,
wide enough to hold uncertainty,
strong enough to bear hope,
tender enough to return, again and again, to the ground we love.

The pigeons know.
They have always known.

And if we are willing,
softening our hearts, opening our breath, trusting the invisible rivers of life,
we can remember, too.

The sky is not elsewhere.
It is here.

Within us.

Waiting.

Chapter 6
The Fierce Love of Parents

The Fragile Beginning

Every life begins in helplessness.

For pigeons, that beginning is often cradled in precarious places, like the lip of a window, the hollow of a rusted beam or the corner of a rooftop forgotten by the world. The nest is not glamorous. It is not fortified or grand. It is often no more than a loose collection of twigs and feathers, arranged quickly, instinctively, held together by hope and habit.

And yet, in this fragile cradle, something astonishing happens: a new being, breathless and blind, enters the world; soft, unfinished and utterly dependent.

The pigeon parent does not look away.
There is no hesitation.
The adult stays, warming, watching and guarding, even in the open air and when rain lashes the eaves and sirens howl beneath the ledges.

In a world of hunger, the cold and rain, predators and indifference, this is an act of radical devotion.
To sit with the vulnerable.
To give warmth.
To wait.

To choose presence over escape.

Building a Nest in a Broken World

Pigeons do not wait for perfection.

They do not demand stillness or peace before beginning the work of nurturing.

They build in the broken places.

On ruined balconies.
On cracked cornices.
Inside forgotten rafters above train stations and alleyways.

With only scraps and instinct, they create a sense of safety.

The nest may be thin.
It may be exposed.
But it is *enough*.

A lesson is whispered beneath feathers and wind about creating a sanctuary where none seems to exist.
About loving amid instability.
About choosing to protect what is precious, even when the world offers no guarantees.

Many of us carry the same challenge.
We parent, protect and care in uncertain times and fractured places, using limited tools and frayed nerves.
We give, not because the conditions are perfect, but because the life before us is real.

The pigeon teaches us this:
Begin anyway.

Build anyway.
Protect anyway.

Even if the world is falling around you, you make a space for something to live.

Feeding from the Heart

There is a particular tenderness in the way pigeons feed their young.

Unlike most birds, pigeons do not bring insects or seeds.
They produce crop milk, a nutrient-rich substance formed within their bodies, which they regurgitate into the mouths of their squabs.
Both parents feed this way, giving not just food but also a piece of themselves.

It is a form of nourishment that blurs the line between sustenance and sacrifice.

To feed someone from your own body, to create nourishment from within.
This is not a gesture of convenience.
It is love made physical.
Love made cellular.

There is something deeply human in this, too.

Parents, caregivers and lovers, all those who have ever given someone else their energy, time, patience and even pain, know this invisible economy.

Love costs us.
And we give anyway.

Not because it is easy.
But because life depends on it.

The Quiet Violence of Care

Love is often imagined as soft.
But real love, the love that protects, defends and endures, has an edge.

Pigeons, so gentle in flight, will *fiercely* defend their nest.
They will beat their wings against intruders, strike with beaks, hiss with startling sharpness.

They are not violent by nature.

But they do not hesitate to become fierce when the life they protect is threatened.

This, too, is love.

It is not cruel.
It is not angry.
It is the focused, embodied refusal to allow harm to what is vulnerable and sacred.

In human life, this kind of love often goes unseen.

It is the mother who stands between her child and a storm.
The father who sacrifices sleep, pride, comfort and time, to keep one more day intact.

The guardian, the teacher, the nurse, the elder, the friend, who repeatedly puts their body and heart in the path of difficulty, without asking for thanks.

There is a violence in that care, not destructive, but determined.

A love that says: *you will not touch this one unless you go through me first.*

This love does not shout its name.
It simply stands its ground.

Preparing to Let Go

All care leads, eventually, to the moment of release.

The young pigeon grows.
Its feathers darken.
It begins to flutter at the edge of the nest, unsure and unsteady, full of invisible longing.

And then, one day, it lifts.

The parent does not chase.
The parent does not beg.

The parent watches.

There is sorrow in this moment.
But there is also triumph.

To raise something strong enough to fly is the greatest triumph of love.
Even if it means watching it disappear into the sky.

The pigeons do not cling.
They prepare.
They feed, protect, warm, and trust until the time comes to say, silently, 'go.'

And in that letting go, a different kind of love is born,
the kind that honours freedom, not just safety.
The kind that holds space instead of possession.

Closing Reflection: The Fierce Grace of Giving Life

Not all love is loud.

Not all devotion is named.

Some love is lived in the quiet dark
on ledges that crumble, in air that bites, under roofs that never promised shelter.

Some love is built from scraps
from time and instinct and a refusal to leave the fragile alone.

Some love is fierce, not in anger, but in the steadiness of care.

It holds the hungry.
It guards the sleep of the small.
It wakes at dawn without thanks.
It gives, not because it is easy, but because it is *right*.

Pigeons do not name their love.
They do not wrap it in language or ritual.
They build it.
They feed it.
They stand beside it in cold wind and in silence.

And then, they let it fly.

This is the shape of the love that sustains the world.

It is the teacher's love.
The elder's love.
The exhausted parent's love.

The invisible, faithful, unspoken love that keeps life going when no one is looking.

It is fierce.
It is tired.
It is quiet.
It is holy.

The pigeons know.
They have always known.

And if we pause long enough to honour them,
to see them not just as birds, but as keepers of ancient love,
we might begin to honour the love within ourselves,
and within those who loved us when we were too small to remember.

Chapter 7

The Language of Wings

A Grammar Before Words

There is a language in the sky that predates grammar.
It speaks not in syllables, but in arcs and spirals.
The flock becomes a sentence; wordless, yet understood.
Pigeons do not translate; they move.

While we name, define and misinterpret, they turn mid-air without command.
Their communication is not obedience, but attunement.
It is not taught. It is lived.

This, too, is language that is older than the tongue.
Immediate. Embodied. Whole.

The Choreography of the Collective

No leader directs the turn.
No order is barked across the wind.
Instead, presence emerges—shared, dynamic, indivisible.
Scientists refer to it as emergent synchrony or distributed leadership.
But the terms fall short.

What unfolds is not mechanical. It is relational.
A murmuration is not a strategy.
It is communion.

It reminds us: belonging does not always require words.
Sometimes, it only asks us to move together.

Movement as Meaning

Language often fails us.
Pigeons communicate with their bodies, and in doing so, they bypass misunderstandings.
In their flight, we see the possibility of understanding without articulation.
Not assertion, but adjustment.
Not ideology, but sensitivity.

Each wingbeat responds not to command, but to the wing beside it.
This is not a submission. It is *response-ability.*
A moral intelligence grounded in perception.

Can we live like this?
Can we move in rhythm with others rather than react?

The Skyborne Encounter

Martin Buber called it the *I–Thou* moment:
Presence that does not seek to define or use, but to meet.

Pigeons embody this.
They do not isolate; they attune.
They do not argue; they enact.

Their syntax is aerial.
Their metaphors are arcs.
Their stanzas spiral.

They write nothing down,
but everything is inscribed in flight.

An Invitation, Not a Command

The flock does not issue commandments.
Only invitation.

To live more responsively.
To sense more finely.
To adjust with grace.

If we could learn even a fragment of this grammar,
perhaps we might rebuild our commons,
not through consensus, but concord.

For now, they rise.
A murmuration in motion.
A body made of many.
No message left; it's only a reminder:
Once and maybe again,
we knew how to move as one.

Closing Reflection: Not all communication is spoken.

Not all connection is forged through words.

Pigeons move together in a rhythm that defies language,
a presence that does not explain itself,
yet is deeply known.

They remind us that meaning can live in gesture,
in breath, in the spaces between.
That harmony is not the result of command,
but of listening, of attunement.

We have learned to speak,
but perhaps we have forgotten how to move with others.
To sense the shift.
To adjust with grace.
To belong without asserting.

The flock offers a different kind of wisdom,
not dominance, not hierarchy,
but shared movement through the uncertainty of air.

If we quieten the noise,
if we soften our separateness,
we might remember how to move as one.
Not in uniformity,
but in communion.

The pigeons do not speak.
But they understand.
And perhaps that is the deeper language after all.

Chapter 8
Hunger and the Search for Enough

The Oldest Language

In every city, under every bench, the story repeats:
A pigeon lands. A crumb glints in the sun. A scramble. One gets it. One keeps searching.
This is not desperation.
It is life.
Hunger is the oldest language; older than names, older than shame.
And pigeons speak it fluently.
Not just as biology, but as being.

We know this language too.
But we've forgotten how to listen.

The Scavenger's Philosophy

Predators dazzle us: lions, hawks, wolves.
But pigeons? They scavenge.
They gather what is left behind.

We see that as lesser.
But pigeons teach a subtler truth:
Survival and even joy can come not from conquest,
but from attentiveness.

To scavenge is to notice.
To take what is already here.
To eat what you need, then fly away.
No hoarding. No spectacle. No shame.
Just enough.

What a rare thing that is.

When Is Enough?

We live in a paradox:
Surrounded by abundance, yet haunted by scarcity.
Overfed, yet undernourished.
Surrounded by stuff, yet aching for worth.

Our hunger has lost its roots.
It is no longer the stomach ache, but the anxiety of not being enough.

Pigeons do not have this confusion.
They eat, rest, coo and sleep.
They stop when satisfied.

Epicurus wrote:
"If you wish to be rich, do not add to your money, but subtract from your desire."

Pigeons live like they already know this.
Their limit is their wisdom.

The Appetites We Inherit

We are born hungry.
For milk, for touch, for attention.
Those hungers mature, but never vanish.
We crave approval, love, and certainty.

But unlike pigeons, we complicate our hunger.
We hide it. We punish it.
Spiritualise it or shame it.

What if we honoured it instead?

The pigeon does not moralise about hunger.
It follows the scent. It adapts. It moves on.
That is not failure. That is faith.

There is something sacred in that persistence.

The Beauty of the Small Meal

Have you ever watched a pigeon peck slowly in the sun,
unbothered by traffic or time?
There is grace in that moment,
not in abundance, but in simplicity.

We are taught to chase grand meaning.
But pigeons show us life is built from small satisfactions:
a crust, a shaft of light, a moment of peace.

Enough is not a number.
It is a feeling.
A moment that whispers: "This is good."

And that, perhaps, is the most radical virtue of all.

Scarcity and Solidarity

Yes, pigeons sometimes fight.
A dozen wings for a single crumb.
Survival is what sharpens them.

But the flock remains.

In scarcity, they do not scatter.
They shift, yield and return.

Yet hunger does not isolate them.
It reminds them of each other.

We, too, wake up hungry.
For food. For love. For meaning.
We can also search together, if we remember how.

Hunger as Humility

To admit hunger is to admit need.
To surrender invincibility.

Pigeons do not pretend.
They follow their hunger with courage.

We, too, can follow;
not mindlessly, but honestly.

We can ask:
Is this true hunger, or fear?
Is this appetite, or a more profound longing?

Sometimes, the world is generous.
Sometimes, it is not.

But still
sometimes the crumb is enough.

Closing Reflection

To be hungry is not a failure.
It is a sign that we are alive.
That we still seek. That we still care.

Pigeons do not apologise for their need.
They do not dress it in pride or disguise it in distraction.
They follow it; quietly, attentively, honestly.

In a world that tells us to accumulate endlessly,
they remind us that sufficiency is a kind of grace.
That peace lives not in excess, but in the gentle pause after enough.

We, too, can learn this rhythm.
To stop. To receive.
To recognise the moment that whispers:
this is good. This is enough.

And in that moment,
we are no longer starving for more.
We are full of presence and simplicity;
with the miracle of being fed
by what already *is*.

Chapter 9
Shelter, Nesting and the Search for Safety

The Hidden Ledge

A ledge.
A corner behind a pipe.
A hollow five-storey-high wall in a city.

This is where pigeons nest.
Not in forests, not in peace.
But amid chaos.
Train stations, rooftops, cathedral eaves.

They build where they can.
Not with grandeur, but with thread.
A few feathers. A plastic string.
And somehow, it is enough.

Shelter is not perfection.
It is presence.

Home for the Restless

Pigeons do not settle.
They live in loops; flying, feeding, circling and waiting.
And yet, they return.

Not always to the same place.
Not always for long.
But return, they do.

Their nests may shift.
But the impulse remains:
To claim a space in a world that never stops moving.

Humans seek the same.
We think safety means locks, deeds, and walls.
But real shelter is not ownership.
It is the quiet knowing that we belong somewhere.
Even if just for now.

The Fragility of Safety

Watch a pigeon's nest:
wind shaking the ledge,
rain soaking the twigs,
people rushing below, unaware.

The world is not kind to the soft.
And yet, the pigeon stays.

We wish for safety to be solid, unchanging, and permanent.
But perhaps it was never meant to be.
Perhaps it is not stillness we need,
but the ability to rebuild.

The pigeon does not mourn the old nest.
It begins again.
It gathers what remains and trusts what comes next.

Safety, then, is not the absence of threat,
but the courage to try again after it passes.

Using What Is Available

Pigeon nests are untidy.
Scraps and strands. Nothing elegant.
But they work.

They are a practice of sufficiency:
use what you find, not what you dream of.

Humans often wait for perfection before we begin;
the perfect home, the perfect moment, the perfect self.
But pigeons remind us:
home is something we make, not something we wait for.

Safety is not a final product.
It is a humble act of faith.

Between Exposure and Sanctuary

City pigeons live in the open.
Half-exposed. Sometimes unwelcome.
And still, they build.

To rest in public,
to love in public,
to need in public;
this is not weakness.

It is bravery.

The pigeon does not hide its needs.
It does not wait for silence.
It does what life requires.

And so can we.

To build safety is not to shield ourselves entirely.
It is to create soft places
in a world that prefers armour.

The Gesture of a Nest

A few twigs. A body's warmth. A quiet return.
That is all it takes.

We imagine safety must be engineered, defended, and locked down.
But pigeons show us another way.

Their nest is a gesture, not a fortress.
A soft refusal to be hardened by the world.

Gaston Bachelard wrote:
"The house shelters daydreaming... It protects the dreamer."

Safety is intimacy.
Not walls.
But warmth.
Not barricades.
But breath.

The pigeon's nest is not functional alone.
It is relational.
It holds coos, closeness and beginnings.

Nesting in Chaos

To build where there is noise.
To rest above subways.
To raise life beside exhaust vents and echoing trains.
This is not madness. It is resilience.

Pigeons nest not where it is quiet,
but where it is possible.

And so can we.

We, too, can nest in noise.
With rituals, with memory, with music.
We can make sanctuaries inside ourselves
and inside each other.

Safety is not the absence of risk.
It is the presence of care.
A corner. A perch. A breath.
A soft return.

Closing Reflection

To nest is to say: this space, however fragile, is enough for now.
To build a shelter is not just to protect life,
but to honour it.

Pigeons remind us that safety is not found.
It is offered.
In gestures. In warmth. In return.

Their nests are not perfect.
They are honest.
And maybe that is all safety has ever asked of us
not to be unbreakable,
but to keep building where life can still breathe.

We are most like them
when we choose presence over perfection,
care over control
and trust over fear.

Not because the world is safe.
But because we are willing to make space for softness
even in the middle of the storm.

Chapter 10

The Fierce Love of Parents

The Stillness That Warms

There is a pigeon, feathers fluffed against the cold,
sitting perfectly still on a hidden ledge.

You may walk past her a hundred times.
You may never see her.
But she is there; brooding, waiting, warming.

Nearby is her mate.
Not absent. Not passive.
He is present.

They guard together.
They take turns.
They return.

Pigeons do not boast of love.
They live it with the fierceness in stillness, relentless in presence.

Partnership as Protection

In the world of pigeons, parenting is shared.
The female broods at night. The male by day.
No drama. No hierarchy. No keeping score.

It is not romantic.
It is necessary.
And in that necessity, a kind of devotion grows.

They share the labour.
Not equally, but faithfully.

Pigeon love is not a sentiment.
It is a structure;
a daily act of endurance, of protection,
of staying.

Parenthood, here, is not a role.
It is a rhythm.

Milk from the Throat

Perhaps the most intimate truth of pigeon parenting is this:
they make milk.

From their throats; both of them.
Crop milk: warm, rich, alive.

Beak to beak, they feed their young not with things gathered,
but with themselves.

This is not about biology.
It is about offering.

To feed from the self.
To nourish from what is generated in response to need.
This is love as transformation.

Not how we give,
but *that* we give
and that in giving, we become something more.

Love Without Applause

No one praises the pigeons.
No monument honours the nest behind a traffic light.
No poem is written for the father cooing in the shadows.

But the love endures.

It is not performed.
It is practised.

In a world obsessed with visibility,
pigeons remind us:
real love is often invisible.

To give without recognition.
To show up without being seen.
To hold space without being held.

This is the quiet miracle
that keeps life going.

The Fear Beneath the Feathers

Pigeon chicks are soft.
Blind. Dependent. Delicate.

And during those weeks in the nest,
the parents are vulnerable too.
Exposed. Still. At risk.

To love is to risk.
To parent is to open yourself to the ache of loss
and stay anyway.

There is no guarantee.
Still, the pigeons guard.
Still, they wait.

To love knowing it might not be enough
and doing it anyway;
this is courage in its truest form.

The Silence of Continuity

When the chick grows;
there is no ceremony.
No farewell.

The parents fly on.
But they return; to each other, to the cycle.
No fanfare. Only rhythm.

We imagine love as fireworks.
But pigeons offer us a quieter truth:

Love as constancy.
Love as repetition.
Love as the thread that survives every unraveling.

What We Learn from the Uncelebrated

Not every act of love is loud.
Some are done in the early hours,
with no witness but the wind.

The pigeon shows us:
to love fiercely is not to feel grand.
It is to keep showing up.
To endure.
To protect.

This is not the love of novels.
It is the love that raises children.
That tends to the fragile.
That continues, even when tired.

And perhaps that is the deepest kind of love we'll ever know.

Closing Reflection

Love does not always declare itself.
It sits, it waits, it warms.
It feeds from its own body.
It defends what cannot yet defend itself.

Pigeons teach us that fierce love
is not about beauty or grandeur.
It is about returning;
again and again, without being asked.

To stay when no one sees.
To give when nothing is guaranteed.
To guard even when it hurts.

This is the love that sustains life.
The kind that builds nests on ledges.
That coos into silence.
That asks for nothing but gives everything.

In the end,
perhaps it is not the dramatic gestures
but the quiet repetitions that shape the soul.

A fierce, ordinary, enduring love.
Just like theirs.
Just like ours.

Chapter 11
Memory Written in Air

Wings That Remember

There are pigeons that remember.
Not with names. Not with stories.
But with wings.

Released far from home,
they circle once
then fly, unwavering, toward a place they haven't seen in
weeks or years.

No map.
No machine.
Only memory.

But what kind of memory is this?

And what might it teach us
about the unseen threads that pull us back
to what matters most?

The Compass Within

Scientists study the homing pigeon's secret.
Magnetic fields.
Low-frequency sounds.
The angle of the sun.
Scent trails in the wind.

And yet
the mystery remains.

Pigeons do not hesitate.
They do not analyse.
They orient.
They return.

Their memory is not stored.
It is embodied.

What if memory is not just recall,
but direction?

Not a ledger of the past,
but a compass for where we're meant to go?

Perhaps we, too, are moved
by things we cannot name:
a smell, a rhythm, a place that feels like home
even if we've never been.

The Body Keeps the Way

Some memory lives in the mind.
Dates. Names.
Stories we can tell.

But another kind lives in the skin.
In the breath.
In the way we turn toward or away
before we understand why.

Pigeons never write.
But they remember.

Humans do, too.

The shoulders that tense with unspoken fear.
The tear that rises with a song.
The hand that knows how to comfort
before the mind can explain.

This is somatic memory;
a kind of knowing that moves faster than words.
A truth that lives in sensation.

The pigeon shows us:
the body is a map.
Trust it.

Remembering Without Story

We are taught to make narratives.
To explain everything.
But pigeons show us another way.

They remember without explaining.
No plot. No confession.
Only return.

Some of our deepest truths
do not live in language.
They move through us like wind.

We remember heartbreak
in the silence before vulnerability.
We remember joy
in the scent of childhood bread.
We remember love
in the moment before a hug.

Not everything needs to be said to be understood.

Some things are remembered
by how we move.

What We Forget and What Remains

Human memory is unreliable.
We forget birthdays.
We misremember faces.
We invent what's missing.

And still
something remains.

A trace.
A feeling.
A pull.

We may forget the conversation,
but remember how it made us feel.
Forget the book,
but remember the shift it caused inside us.

Memory is not a filing cabinet.
It is a garden.
Growing. Fading. Blooming.
Overgrown in places.
Alive.

Pigeons do not remember everything.
But they remember enough to find their way.

So can we.

Carriers of Memory

Once, pigeons were messengers.
Wartime letters.
Urgent news.
Hope tucked under wings.

Even now,
they seem to carry something more;
not in ink,
but in presence.

They remind us
that we, too, are carriers of memory.

The stories of our ancestors.
The instincts of our childhood.
The invisible echoes
that guide how we touch, speak, stay, or leave.

We carry what we do not know.
And we deliver it
through how we live.

Memory as Belonging

Why do pigeons return?
Not because they are told.
Not because it makes sense.

They return
because it is home.
Even when home is invisible.

In a world that scatters us,
memory ties us to belonging.
A scent. A song. A familiar gaze.

Simone Weil wrote:
"To be rooted is perhaps the most important and least recognised need of the human soul."

Pigeons root not in the ground,
but in the air.
In memory.

And we can, too.

Not all homes are places.
Some are people.
Some are ways of being we once knew and forgot.

And remembering, truly remembering,
is not about looking back.
It is about becoming again.

Closing Reflection

Memory does not always come in words.
Sometimes it comes in motion.
In the feeling of going the right way
before you know where it leads.

Pigeons do not tell stories.
They trace them in the sky.
In circles.
In returns.

They teach us that remembering is not just what we recall,
but how we live,
how we turn toward what matters,
how we keep coming back.

We may forget the details.
But we know the direction.
We know the pull.

There is a memory inside you
older than your thoughts
that knows where you belong,
even when you don't.

Trust that.

Because sometimes,
the body knows the way
long before the mind can follow.

Chapter 12

Risk, Trust and the Leap

The Moment Before Flight

A pigeon on a ledge is still.
It leans. Shuffles. Wings twitch.
Then
the leap.

For a breath of time, it does not fly.
It falls.

And what carries it in that moment
is not certainty,
but trust.

Not in the air.
Not in the world.
But in itself.

Every flight begins with a letting go.

The Insecurity of Living

The world is not safe.
Streets. Predators.
Sudden movements. Changing skies.

Pigeons live with risk.
They do not deny it.
They do not wait for it to disappear.

They leap.

If they were ruled by fear,
they would never leave the ledge.

To live is to risk.
To stay open. To start again.
To speak. To rest. To love.

The alternative to risk
is not safety.
It is stagnation.

And pigeons choose flight.

The Necessity of Trust

Wings are not enough.
Flight requires trust
that the body knows,
that the air will meet you,
that motion itself will find rhythm.

Trust is not the absence of doubt.
It is the movement through it.

Each pigeon leaps without guarantees.
Each human act of change has the same effect.

We leave the familiar.
We risk heartbreak.
We speak truths that may not be received.

To trust is not to know.
It is to go anyway.

Not recklessness,
but a philosophy of movement.

Risk as Aliveness

We frame risk as danger.
But it is also a pulse.
A sign of life touching its edge.

Pigeons take micro-risks daily,
weaving through crowds,
navigating traffic,
landing near strangers.

Their survival depends not on stillness,
but on motion.

So does ours.

Growth asks for discomfort.
Change asks for awkwardness.
No evolution without exposure.
No flight without falling first.

To live fully is to risk fully.
To be changed by what you cannot yet name.

To leap.

The Flight That Finds Us

Pigeons do not glide off gracefully.
They push.
Wings slap.
Bodies strain.

The beginning is effort.
No elegance. Just motion.

And then
lift.

The wind joins.
The rhythm returns.
The body aligns.

This is the arc of every bold act:
The first trembling word.
The first awkward note.
The first page of something true.

There is no perfect start.
Only the leap.
And then,
perhaps,
the wings.

Trusting Invisible Paths

Pigeons do not always see where they are going.
Still, they move.

They follow winds they cannot measure.
They trust instincts honed by experience and embodied memory.

We are taught to map everything.
To wait until we know.

But some paths only appear in motion.
Some truths only rise when we leap.

Kierkegaard wrote:
"To dare is to lose one's footing momentarily. Not to dare is to lose oneself."

Pigeons dare.
And so can we.

The Courage of the Small Leap

Not every leap is grand.
Some are quiet.

To rise from bed when your heart aches.
To say *"I'm not sure."*
To begin again.
To be held.

These, too, are flights.

Pigeons remind us:
it is not the distance that matters,
but the decision to move.

To release the ledge.
To fall before you rise.
To trust that something in you still knows how.

Even if you falter,
you can begin again.

Flight is not a one-time act.
It is a rhythm.
A return.
A remembering:

You were always meant for the air.

Closing Reflection

The leap is never tidy.
It stumbles. It shakes.
It begins before you're ready.

But every act of becoming
starts this way.

Pigeons don't wait for perfect conditions.
They move.
Even when the wind is uncertain.
Even when the ledge feels safer.

They remind us:
to live is to leap.

Trust is not a promise of ease.
It is the quiet agreement to try again.
To push into the air you cannot see.
To believe that wings will find their way.

You will not always be certain.
But you do not need to be.
You only need to move.

And the rest;
the rhythm, the lift,
the grace;
will meet you in motion.

Chapter 13

Fragile Bodies, Immortal Stories

The Body That Endures

A pigeon is not built to impress.
Its bones are hollow.
Its wings, modest.
Its colours easily lost in shadow and dust.

And yet,
it endures.

Not with grandeur,
but with quiet resilience.

It adapts.
It returns.
It remains.

Not in monuments,
but in memories.

Its body is fragile.
But its presence is lasting.

The Bird in the Ruins

In the trenches of war,
when words could not pass and men fell silent,
it was pigeons who flew.

Through fire.
Through gas.
Through the smoke of dying worlds.

Cher Ami, wounded, blinded, shot,
still delivered the message that saved 200 lives.
She flew on, broken but unstoppable.

Her body was shattered.
Her story was not.

This is the paradox of the pigeon:
so easily crushed,
yet somehow eternal.

What kind of strength refuses to disappear?

The Memory in the Walls

Cities remember pigeons.

Not in ceremonies,
but in corners.
In the dust of ledges.
In the soft stain of wings on statues.

They roost where emperors once ruled.
They coo in cathedrals.
They fly through train stations,
marking the rhythm of cities
with breath and movement.

They are not owned.
And yet they belong everywhere.

Their presence is not performance.
It is persistence.
A whisper against the roar of progress:
We are still here.

The Fragility We Flee

Humans fear fragility.
We armour ourselves,
with certainty, with size, with status.

But pigeons show us another kind of strength:
to live open.
To carry tenderness through concrete.
To rise, again and again,
while still soft.

They are injured
and they still forage.

They are ignored
and they still return.

They do not apologise for being delicate.
They move forward anyway.

And perhaps that is what it means
to be human, too.

To carry both pain and possibility
in the same breath.

Myths in Feathers

Long before cities,
pigeons flew through myth.

Sacred to Inanna.
Symbols of Aphrodite.
Messengers of the divine.
Bearers of the Holy Spirit.

Not the strongest.
Not the fiercest.
But the most constant.

The pigeon became a vessel
for peace,
for endurance,
for the invisible thread of meaning
that connects us to something greater.

To be mythic is not to dominate.
It is to remain.

The Story That Outlives the Body

A pigeon's life is short.
And yet,
it leaves a trace.

On buildings.
On sky.
On memory.

So do we.

Our bodies wear down.
But what we give:
how we stand,
how we love,
how we choose,
becomes a story that outlives the self.

Not in statues.
But in echoes.

In the laughter of a child.
In the phrase a friend repeats.
In the moments where we mattered.

Immortality is not glory.
It is grace.

It is a flight that leaves an imprint
no one else can replicate.

Closing Reflection

The world rarely celebrates the soft.
But it remembers the steady.

Pigeons do not roar.
They do not reign.
But they return.

They mark time not with spectacle,
but with presence.

And in doing so,
they remind us that it is not strength
that makes something last,
but meaning.

To live with vulnerability.
To show up anyway.
To keep flying through wind and fire
and silence;
this is how stories are made.

We are all breakable.
But we are not broken.

And if we live well,
if we love deeply,
we, too, will leave
a quiet imprint
that does not fade.

Chapter 14
The Wisdom of Non-Importance

No one becomes a pigeon.

Children don't dream of it, and countries don't fly its image on flags. It is not a mascot for greatness or a metaphor for victory.

It is simply there.

Pecking at crumbs. Coexisting. Daring to survive in the margins of human life.

And in that, it may be the wisest of all birds.

Because the pigeon does not seek importance.
And yet, it endures.
It thrives.
It *matters*.

Without ever needing to prove it.

The Ego That Doesn't Arrive

Pigeons do not strut like peacocks.
They do not soar like hawks.
They do not sing like nightingales.

They live without spectacle. They make no grand claims.

Their existence is a quiet rejection of what we are so often taught to chase: recognition, prestige and uniqueness.

The pigeon says: To b*e and not to be seen.*

How different would our lives feel if we weren't trying to be important? If we let go of being known, admired and approved?

Would we suffer less?
Would we fly lighter?

In a world hooked on attention, the pigeon invites us to disappear and still belong.

Humility with Wings

We often confuse humility with self-deprecation. But true humility is not thinking less of yourself; it is thinking *of yourself less*.

It is existing without the obsession of image.

Pigeons do not look in mirrors, brand themselves, or ask if they are special.

They do what life calls them to do.

They feed. They fly. They nest.
They live in rhythm with the moment.

And in this humble, uncelebrated, unshared pattern, they embody a kind of peace that eludes even the most praised among us.

Because freedom is not just the ability to fly.
It is the ability to fly without needing to be watched.

The Lightness of Letting Go

To be non-important is not to be meaningless. It is to be *free of the weight of performance.*

The pigeon is not trying to win, impress or survive more than necessary.

It lets the world pass by, yet remains a part of it.

This is a form of wisdom: letting go of the struggle to prove your worth.

To be as you are, grey, quiet and soft and to find that it is *enough.*

The philosopher Lao Tzu wrote:
"When you are content to be yourself and don't compare or compete, everyone will respect you."

Perhaps not everyone will *notice* you.
But respect, in its deepest form, does not come from applause. It comes from living in truth.

The City's Companion

We call them *"rats with wings,"* and still they stay.

We try to shoo them off ledges, but they still return.

There is something deeply unshakable in their presence, not because they force it, but because they do not resist being dismissed.

They live alongside us without asking for permission.

There is a strange beauty in this refusal to matter more.

Because in doing so, they make space for others to matter.

They are background creatures, yet they are included in every photograph of a square, every walk through the park, and every quiet rooftop sunset.

They are woven into our cities not as symbols, but as *companions*.

Their humility makes them belong.

Being Without Needing to Become

In the modern world, we are conditioned to 'become' something: to rise, establish a brand, and grow exponentially.

But pigeons offer a counter-practice: *being*.

They do not become better pigeons.
They do not evolve toward fame.

They live their one small life with full participation and with no self-importance.

And in that, they reflect a profound spiritual truth: that meaning is not tied to magnitude.

The sun warms the pigeon as it does the falcon.
The wind lifts its wings with the same indifference.
The Earth does not distinguish.

There is a profound wisdom in accepting one's smallness.
Not as a flaw, but as a form of belonging.

Closing Reflection

The pigeon lives where we live.
Walks where we walk.
Eats what we drop.

And in doing so, it turns the overlooked into the essential.

It reminds us that nothing is beneath attention and that there is a sacredness in what the world often overlooks.

In many spiritual traditions, the divine is found not in grand temples, but in the small acts of daily life: sweeping a floor, lighting a candle or feeding a bird.

To notice a pigeon, to really *see* it, is to practise reverence.

Not for it alone, but for the entire fabric of the unnoticed world.

The world that keeps turning, even when we are not watching.

The world that *is*, without needing to be important.

Just like the pigeon.

Just like us, when we remember.

Conclusion
The Flight We Share

You've made it this far, not by soaring through grand theories, but by walking beside a bird often ignored. Neither exotic nor rare, the pigeon has guided us through alleys and rooftops, through memories and migrations, offering lessons in patience and softness, and connecting us to cities and spirits. Not because it is heroic. But because it is present. And that is the point.

To notice the pigeon is to notice life again, unfiltered, unpolished and unassuming. The pigeon survives by blending in in a world obsessed with visibility and validation. It asks for nothing, yet teaches everything: how to return to ourselves, adapt without fuss, love with quiet intensity, and remain gentle in a harsh world.

This was never intended to be a book about birds. It is about how to live.
More attentively. More humbly. More truthfully.

Each feathered lesson pointed back to us:
To our forgotten homes.
To our hunger for enough.
To our fragile bodies and immortal longings.
To the risk of loving and the grace of not needing to be important.

The pigeon doesn't perform for our admiration, and maybe that's what makes it sacred.
Its wisdom isn't shouted; it coos.

So take these pages not as a doctrine, but as a nest. Temporary, light and real. A place to pause before your next flight.

Carry what you need. Leave what you don't. And when the sky calls, rise, pigeon-hearted.

After all, the bird you barely see… might just be the part of yourself you most need to remember.

Introduction to the Companion Guide

This companion guide provides a quiet space to return to, echoing the voices that have accompanied us throughout the book. Each chapter was shaped by the presence of a philosopher whose work deepens, anchors or expands the theme it carries. These entries are not academic profiles but living invitations: to see these thinkers not as distant authorities, but as fellow travellers, people who asked questions, wrestled with uncertainty and tried to describe the shape of being alive.

You will find here a brief biography of each philosopher, a summary of their core ideas, a reflection on how their thought is woven into the chapter they anchor and a few words of theirs that still resonate. For those who are moved to follow these voices further, each entry concludes with a suggestion for additional reading.

Let this guide be a window, part mirror, part map, for wherever your thinking wants to go.

Ch.	Current Title	Philosopher Referenced
1	The Art of Returning Home	Søren Kierkegaard
2	The Patience of the Pavement	Marcus Aurelius
3	Softness as Strength	Lao Tzu
4	The Grace of the Ordinary	Brother Lawrence
5	The Gift of Wings	Rainer Maria Rilke
6	The Fierce Love of Parents	Simone de Beauvoir
7	The Language of Wings	Martin Buber

Ch.	Current Title	Philosopher Referenced
8	Hunger and the Search for Enough	Epicurus
9	Shelter, Nesting and the Search for Safety	Gaston Bachelard
10	Risk, Trust and the Leap	Søren Kierkegaard
11	Memory Written in Air	Simone Weil
12	Fragile Bodies, Immortal Stories	Albert Camus
13	The Wisdom of Non-Importance	Lao Tzu
14	The Flight We Share (Conclusion)	— (No philosopher added)

The Philosophers we have met:

Søren Kierkegaard – The Art of Returning Home

Søren Kierkegaard (1813–1855) was a Danish philosopher, theologian and poet widely regarded as the father of existentialism. Writing against the rationalism and religiosity of his time, Kierkegaard emphasised individual subjectivity, inwardness and the necessity of personal choice. His work explores anxiety, despair, faith and the leap into authentic selfhood.

In the chapter *"The Art of Returning Home,"* Kierkegaard's thought frames home as not a fixed place but a task of becoming. To 'return' is not nostalgic but existential; it means stepping into the challenge of living as one's true self, beyond social masks and comforting illusions. For Kierkegaard, this journey involves confronting dread and despair not as enemies but as signs of a more profound transformation.

He reminds us that homecoming begins within. The *'leap of faith'* is required not into dogma, but into the uncertainty of self-trust and spiritual freedom. He wrote, *"The most painful state of being is remembering the future, particularly the one you'll never have."* His melancholy brilliance insists that courage is born not from certainty, but from choosing to live meaningfully in spite of doubt.

Further reading: Fear and Trembling, The Sickness Unto Death, Either/Or, The Concept of Anxiety

Marcus Aurelius – The Patience of the Pavement

Marcus Aurelius (121–180 CE) was a Roman emperor and a Stoic philosopher. He is best known for his journal, Meditations, which he wrote during his military campaigns. Despite ruling one of history's most powerful empires, Marcus approached life with humility and introspection. His Stoicism taught that external circumstances are beyond our control, but our inner response is our domain.

In *"The Patience of the Pavement,"* Marcus Aurelius anchors the worn, grounded and enduring pavement metaphor. For him, patience is not passive waiting but the disciplined practice of accepting what is while continuing to walk forward with integrity. The Stoic principle of *amor fati*, the love of one's fate, urges us to meet the ordinary with equanimity and purpose.

He reminds us to attend to the moment without complaint, perform small acts well, and endure hardship gracefully. He wrote, *"You have power over your mind, not outside events. Realise this and you will find strength."* The pavement may not glitter, but it holds the quiet nobility of one who walks faithfully in chaos.

Further reading: Meditations, Pierre Hadot's *The Inner Citadel*, Donald Robertson's *How to Think Like a Roman Emperor*

Lao Tzu – Softness as Strength

Although some debate his historical existence, Lao Tzu (6th century BCE) is the legendary Chinese sage credited with writing the *Tao Te Ching*, the foundational text of Taoist philosophy. His teachings revolve around harmony with the Tao, the mysterious, flowing order of nature and emphasise non-resistance, simplicity and the paradox of strength through softness.

In *"Softness as Strength,"* Lao Tzu's thought anchors the idea that what yields endures. Like water carving through rock or the wind that shapes mountains, true strength lies in flexibility and humility. He challenges the Western ideal of power as dominance, offering a path of quiet, unobtrusive influence instead.

Lao Tzu's wisdom invites us to stop striving and start flowing, to act without force, speak without argument and move without resistance. He wrote, *"Nothing in the world is as soft and yielding as water. Yet for dissolving the hard and inflexible, nothing can surpass it."* His vision turns the world upside down and, in doing so, sets it right.

Further reading: Tao Te Ching (Stephen Mitchell or Ursula Le Guin translations), Chuang Tzu's *Inner Chapters*, Benjamin Hoff's *The Tao of Pooh*

Brother Lawrence – The Grace of the Ordinary

Brother Lawrence (1614–1691) was a French Carmelite lay brother best known for his posthumously published work, *The Practice of the Presence of God*. A humble man who spent most of his life working in a monastery kitchen, he believed that spiritual enlightenment could be found not in dramatic acts or sacred rituals, but in the quiet attention to everyday tasks.

In *"The Grace of the Ordinary,"* Brother Lawrence reminds us that the sacred is always close, woven into the simple acts of daily life. For him, peeling potatoes or sweeping floors could be acts of divine communion when performed with love and awareness. His spirituality was marked by cheerfulness, steadiness and deep inner peace.

He wrote, *"We ought not to be weary of doing little things for the love of God, who regards not the greatness of the work but the love with which it is performed."* Brother Lawrence offers the soft revolution of presence in a world that worships spectacle, where grace blooms in the smallest things.

Further reading: The Practice of the Presence of God, Henri Nouwen's *Discernment*, Kathleen Norris's *The Quotidian Mysteries*

Rainer Maria Rilke – The Gift of Wings

Rainer Maria Rilke (1875–1926) was a Bohemian-Austrian poet and writer, celebrated for his lyrical intensity and exploration of solitude, beauty and transformation. His *Letters to a Young Poet*, Duino Elegies, and Sonnets to Orpheus express a profound trust in the inner life and a reverent openness to mystery.

In *"The Gift of Wings,"* Rilke's poetic vision becomes a metaphor for inner unfolding. Wings are not a means of escape but a symbol of self-becoming, fragile, earned and quietly powerful. Rilke believed that the significant challenges in life — loss, love, and longing — are not problems to be solved, but thresholds to be crossed.

He wrote, *"Perhaps all the dragons in our lives are princesses who are only waiting to see us act, just once, with beauty and courage."* Rilke reminds us that flight begins not in control, but in surrender to the unknown, the beautiful and the painful. In trusting our wings, we begin to rise.

Further reading: Letters to a Young Poet, Duino Elegies, Sonnets to Orpheus, Robert Bly's *A Little Book on the Human Shadow*

Simone de Beauvoir – The Fierce Love of Parents

Simone de Beauvoir (1908–1986) was a French existentialist philosopher, writer and feminist. Best known for *"The Second Sex,"* she examined the cultural construction of womanhood and our ethical responsibilities in our relationships. As a close collaborator of Jean-Paul Sartre, her work bridges the realms of existential freedom and relational ethics.

In *"The Fierce Love of Parents,"* de Beauvoir offers a lens for understanding parental love as a complex ethical act. Love, for her, is not ownership but affirmation of the other's freedom. To truly love a child is to nurture without control, to guide without erasing their becoming.

She wrote, *"To will oneself moral and to will oneself free are one and the same decision."* The fierce love of parents is not just self-sacrifice, but also standing beside a growing soul with courage, humility and commitment. De Beauvoir teaches that love matures when it relinquishes itself.

Further reading: The Second Sex, Ethics of Ambiguity, Kate Kirkpatrick's *Becoming Beauvoir*

Martin Buber – The Language of Wings

Martin Buber (1878–1965) was an Austrian-Israeli philosopher and theologian best known for his philosophy of dialogue, expressed in his seminal work *I and Thou*. He argued that human existence is defined by relationships, not only with people, but with nature, God and the world.

In *"The Language of Wings,"* Buber's thought voices the relational space between beings. The wing becomes a metaphor for the soul's capacity to reach, listen to and meet the other in a sacred way. For Buber, genuine connection occurs in the I-Thou moment, an encounter devoid of objectification or utilitarianism.

He wrote, *"All real living is meeting."* This chapter explores how we speak without words, how presence creates flight and how mutual recognition transforms solitude into shared sky. Buber invites us to move beyond separation, into the poetry of relationship, where even silence becomes a language of its own.

Further reading: I and Thou, The Way of Man, Maurice Friedman's *Martin Buber: The Life of Dialogue*

Epicurus – Hunger and the Search for Enough

Epicurus (341–270 BCE) was an ancient Greek philosopher who founded a school known as *The Garden*, where philosophy was a way of life dedicated to simple pleasures, friendship and the pursuit of tranquillity (*ataraxia*). Often mischaracterised as a hedonist, Epicurus taught that the greatest pleasures are modest and rooted in the absence of pain and fear.

In *"Hunger and the Search for Enough,"* Epicurus reorients our understanding of desire. In this view, hunger is not something to be suppressed or endlessly indulged, but instead listened to, an invitation to discern what is truly needed. He distinguished between natural and unnecessary desires, reminding us that many of our longings are artificially created.

He wrote, *"If you wish to be rich, do not add to your money, but subtract from your desire."* The search for enough is a philosophical act: a return to simplicity, gratitude and self-liberation from the illusion that more will complete us.

Further reading: Letter to Menoeceus, Diogenes Laërtius' *Lives of the Philosophers*, Emily Austin's *Living for Pleasure: An Epicurean Guide to Life*

Gaston Bachelard – Shelter, Nesting and the Search for Safety

Gaston Bachelard (1884–1962) was a French philosopher and poet of imagination who blended science, poetry and phenomenology. In his seminal work, *The Poetics of Space*, Bachelard examined how intimate spaces, such as houses, corners and nests, shape our dreams and memories. He believed that imagination is not an escape from reality but a way of deepening it.

In *"Shelter, Nesting and the Search for Safety,"* Bachelard's reflections guide us toward the inward experience of space. A home is not simply a structure; it is a vessel for reverie, a haven for the soul. Nests, shells and drawers become symbols of safety, belonging, and being enclosed gently by the world.

He wrote, *"The house shelters daydreaming, the house protects the dreamer, the house allows one to dream in peace."* Bachelard reminds us that proper safety comes from walls and the poetic intimacy we weave within them.

Further reading: The Poetics of Space, The Psychoanalysis of Fire, Water and Dreams

Søren Kierkegaard – Risk, Trust and the Leap

Kierkegaard (1813–1855) reappears here and takes us deeper into the heart of existential risk. In "Risk, Trust and the Leap," we move from the homecoming of self to the tension of decision, when one must leap without guarantee. Kierkegaard's 'leap of faith' is not irrationality but the bold commitment to a future that cannot be proven in advance.

For him, trust is not naïve; it is an act of profound courage. The leap is spiritual and personal, whether it involves love, vocation or belief. He wrote, *"To dare is to lose one's footing momentarily. Not to dare is to lose oneself."* The risk is not failure, but stagnation.

This chapter examines how we reach those pivotal moments when certainty fails and we must act nonetheless. Kierkegaard urges us to leap, not because we know what awaits, but because in leaping, we become.

Further reading: Fear and Trembling, The Concept of Anxiety and Clare Carlisle's *Philosopher of the Heart*

Simone Weil – Memory Written in Air

Simone Weil (1909–1943) was a French philosopher, mystic and political activist known for her profound insights into suffering, attention and grace. A thinker of immense moral depth, Weil lived what she taught, working in factories, aiding resistance movements and embracing a life of voluntary poverty. Her writings draw from philosophy, Christian mysticism and classical thought.

In *"Memory Written in Air,"* Weil's unique vision helps us explore memory as something delicate, almost intangible, like breath or birdsong. For her, proper attention is a spiritual act, and memory that arises from such attention is marked not by possession, but by reverence. She taught that suffering becomes redemptive only when we consent to look at it without turning away.

She wrote, *"Attention is the rarest and purest form of generosity."* Memory, then, is not about clinging to the past, but about opening ourselves to what was, allowing it to shape us without imprisoning us. It drifts like air that is ungraspable yet essential.

Further reading: Gravity and Grace, Waiting for God, Simone Weil: An Anthology, edited by Sian Miles

Albert Camus – Fragile Bodies, Immortal Stories

Albert Camus (1913–1960) was a French-Algerian writer, philosopher and journalist who received the Nobel Prize in Literature in 1957. Known for his exploration of the absurd, the tension between humanity's desire for meaning and the world's indifference, Camus believed that the response to absurdity must be rebellion, not despair.

In *"Fragile Bodies, Immortal Stories,"* Camus reminds us that though the body perishes, the story lives on. His myth of Sisyphus, the man condemned to roll a boulder up a hill forever, symbolises human perseverance. Camus does not ask us to deny suffering, but to affirm life in the face of it.

He wrote, *"In the depth of winter, I finally learned that within me there lay an invincible summer."* In telling stories, we claim dignity over our mortality. The body may falter, but meaning is shaped in how we live, remember, and share the flame with others.

Further reading: The Myth of Sisyphus, The Plague, The Rebel, The Stranger

Lao Tzu – The Wisdom of Non-Importance

In *"The Wisdom of Non-Importance,"* Lao Tzu returns to challenge the ego's yearning for recognition. Taoist thought values the unnoticed, the ordinary, the unseen. Lao Tzu reminds us that the most potent forces, water, wind and emptiness, do not need applause. In Taoism, what does not strive becomes what endures.

This chapter is an invitation to humility, to the peace that arises when we relinquish the need to be important. Lao Tzu wrote, *"When you are content to be yourself and don't compare or compete, everyone will respect you."* The goal is not erasure of self, but freedom from the burden of self-importance.

Living in harmony with the Tao means understanding that real power moves in silence. Just as the roots nourish the unseen tree, wisdom also thrives in obscurity. Lao Tzu reminds us that anonymity can be its form of spiritual abundance.

Further reading: Tao Te Ching (translations by Stephen Mitchell, Ursula Le Guin), *The Book of Chuang Tzu*, Deng Ming-Dao's *Everyday Tao*

The Flight We Share – A Concluding Reflection

This final chapter departs from a single philosophical anchor to honour the multiplicity of voices, insights and quiet awakenings throughout the book. "The Flight We Share" is not guided by one thinker but by the accumulated weight and lift of all those who have come before, those who dared to question, observe, feel and write.

By now, the reader has walked with the solitude of Kierkegaard, the clarity of Aurelius, the tenderness of de Beauvoir and the mystery of Lao Tzu. This is not the end of a path but a recognition: we never fly alone. Even when our journeys feel singular, they are shaped by a shared sky, language, and longing.

In this closing view, philosophy is not an abstract theory, but a lived rhythm; an embodied invitation to choose our steps, remember our wings, and honour the others who soar beside us.

No single quote can conclude this journey. Instead, the reader is left with a question: *What flight are you ready to take now?*

Further reading: Your reflections, your life and the philosophers you meet next.

References & Further Reading

This book is not a scholarly work, but rather a quiet conversation with thinkers whose words and lives have shaped its pages. For readers who wish to explore further alongside them, here is a list of the primary sources and companion works that inspired each chapter's gentle philosophy.

Primary Philosophical Works

- **Søren Kierkegaard**
  Fear and Trembling, The Sickness Unto Death, Either/Or, The Concept of Anxiety
- **Marcus Aurelius**
  Meditations
- **Lao Tzu**
  Tao Te Ching (translations by Stephen Mitchell or Ursula K. Le Guin)
- **Brother Lawrence**
  The Practice of the Presence of God
- **Rainer Maria Rilke**
  Letters to a Young Poet, Duino Elegies, Sonnets to Orpheus
- **Simone de Beauvoir**
  The Second Sex, The Ethics of Ambiguity
- **Martin Buber**
  I and Thou
- **Epicurus**
  Letter to Menoeceus, Diogenes Laërtius' *Lives of Eminent Philosophers*
- **Gaston Bachelard**
  The Poetics of Space

- **Simone Weil**
  Gravity and Grace, Waiting for God
- **Albert Camus**
  The Myth of Sisyphus, The Plague, The Rebel, The Stranger

Secondary & Interpretive Texts

- Pierre Hadot — *The Inner Citadel: The Meditations of Marcus Aurelius*
- Donald Robertson — *How to Think Like a Roman Emperor*
- Benjamin Hoff — *The Tao of Pooh*
- Henri Nouwen — *Discernment: Reading the Signs of Daily Life*
- Kathleen Norris — *The Quotidian Mysteries: Laundry, Liturgy and "Women's Work"*
- Robert Bly — *A Little Book on the Human Shadow*
- Kate Kirkpatrick — *Becoming Beauvoir: A Life*
- Maurice Friedman — *Martin Buber: The Life of Dialogue*
- Emily Austin — *Living for Pleasure: An Epicurean Guide to Life*
- Clare Carlisle — *Philosopher of the Heart: The Restless Life of Søren Kierkegaard*
- Deng Ming-Dao — *Everyday Tao: Living with Balance and Harmony*
- Siân Miles (ed.) — *Simone Weil: An Anthology*

Additional Context & Inspiration

This book also draws quietly from shared knowledge about the natural history and cultural symbolism of pigeons: their remarkable homing instinct, their role as messengers in war, and their presence as humble companions in myth, folklore and city life.

A Final Word

Let these works be a soft trail of breadcrumbs rather than a syllabus, but a nest to return to, and from which to retake flight. May they deepen the quiet philosophy you now carry forward.

www.ingramcontent.com/pod-product-compliance
Lightning Source LLC
Chambersburg PA
CBHW052055070526
44584CB00017B/2192